# How to Live Like a Fairy

## Life Lessons from the Fairy Realm

*Joy McGuire*

Pure Fate Publishing

*Dedicated to the love of my life, Tom, who keeps me grounded and inspires me to be a better person. I couldn't do any of this without him.* ❤️

HOW TO LIVE LIKE A FAIRY

Copyright © 2023 by Joy McGuire

ISBN: 978-1-7332350-1-3

# Introduction

The Universe is governed by unseen energy forces. Some of these energies can be called Fairies.

Whether you call them Elves or Pixies, Elementals or Spirits, whether you are a believer or not, whether you can see them or not; there is much to be learned if we attune to the energetic forces of the Fairy realms.

Fairies are playful and creative beings, and they can encourage us to tap into our own inner child and embrace our sense of wonder and magic.

Following are some uplifting affirmations inspired by these whimsical beings to help you tap into your own creativity and joy - and the boundless potential of your own magical being.

When you dream, dream BIG.
Know that anything is possible.
Take inspiration from the Fairies,
who never let their diminutive
presence limit the size of their
accomplishments.

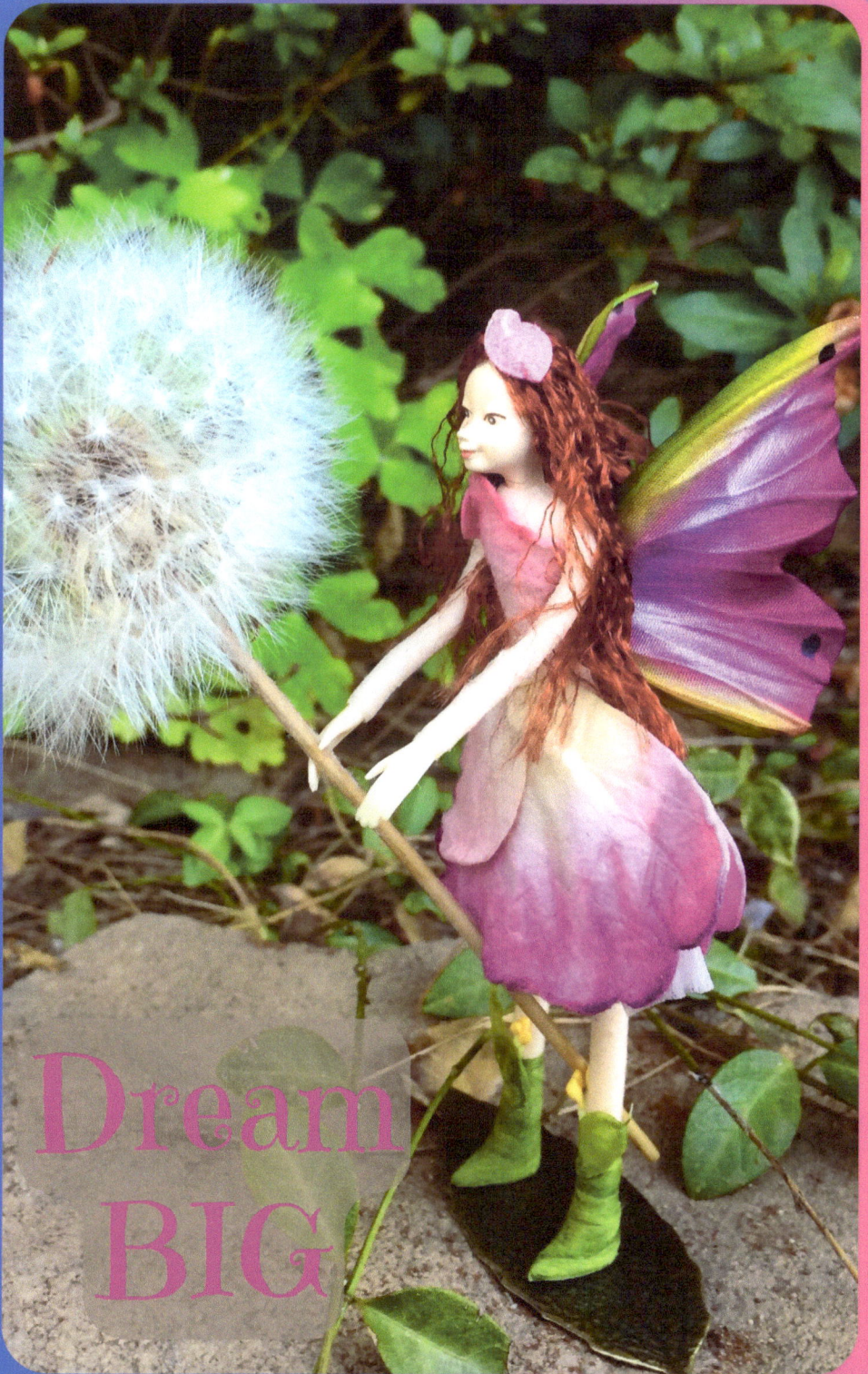

Dream
BIG

Breathe in the fresh air and feel the energies of the earth as you can only do outside. Fairies understand the magic of the great outdoors and thrive when out in nature.

# Spend Time Outdoors

Intuition is the sixth sense and as powerful as touch or taste. Fairies rely instinctively on their intuition. Sadly, humans have forgotten to trust their gut feelings. The good news is that anyone can increase this skill with practice.

# Trust Yourself

Taking time to 'smell the roses' is not just a cliché, but a reminder for us to slow down and appreciate what is around us. Fairies are busy creatures, but they never pass up a chance to inhale the sweet fragrance of a flower.

# Smell the Flowers

It can be scary to venture out of our comfort zones, but taking a chance on something different or embarking on an adventurous journey can be incredibly rewarding. New experiences help us grow as humans and bring us together. Adventure is the basis of life for many fairies.

# Be Adventurous

Make new friends - but keep the old. As the song says: "one is silver and the other gold". New friends can provide us with fresh experiences and new lessons to learn. Old friends can teach us about ourselves, or watch our backs, but mostly - all friends are fun!

# Make Friends

Be a hugger of trees!
Recognize that trees and
plants provide us food and
shelter, clean our air, and
beautify our surroundings.
Not only do Fairies love to
live in or around trees, but
they love to communicate
with them as well.

Hug a Tree

Life can be all too serious at times. That's when it's helpful to return to our childlike innocence. Peter Pan's motto was 'Never Grow Up' and while that's not possible in the human realm (without Pixie dust), it never hurts to incorporate some playful fun into our daily realities.

# Stay Playful

17

Spending time with like-minded people reduces stress. Friends are there for us to laugh or cry with, never judging, just loving. Good friends make life more enjoyable, which is why Fairies love to spend time with their Flutter.

Surround Yourself
with Friends

Quieting the mind can help us hear so much. Taking some time alone for personal reflection helps our body as much as our soul. Fairies rarely remain still, but they know the importance of occasional introspection.

# Enjoy Quiet
# Moments Alone

Dance alone as if nobody's watching, or dance in groups, or have a slow dance with your special someone. Moving the body to the rhythm of music nourishes the soul. Fairies understand the magic of melodies, and have been known to dance all night long.

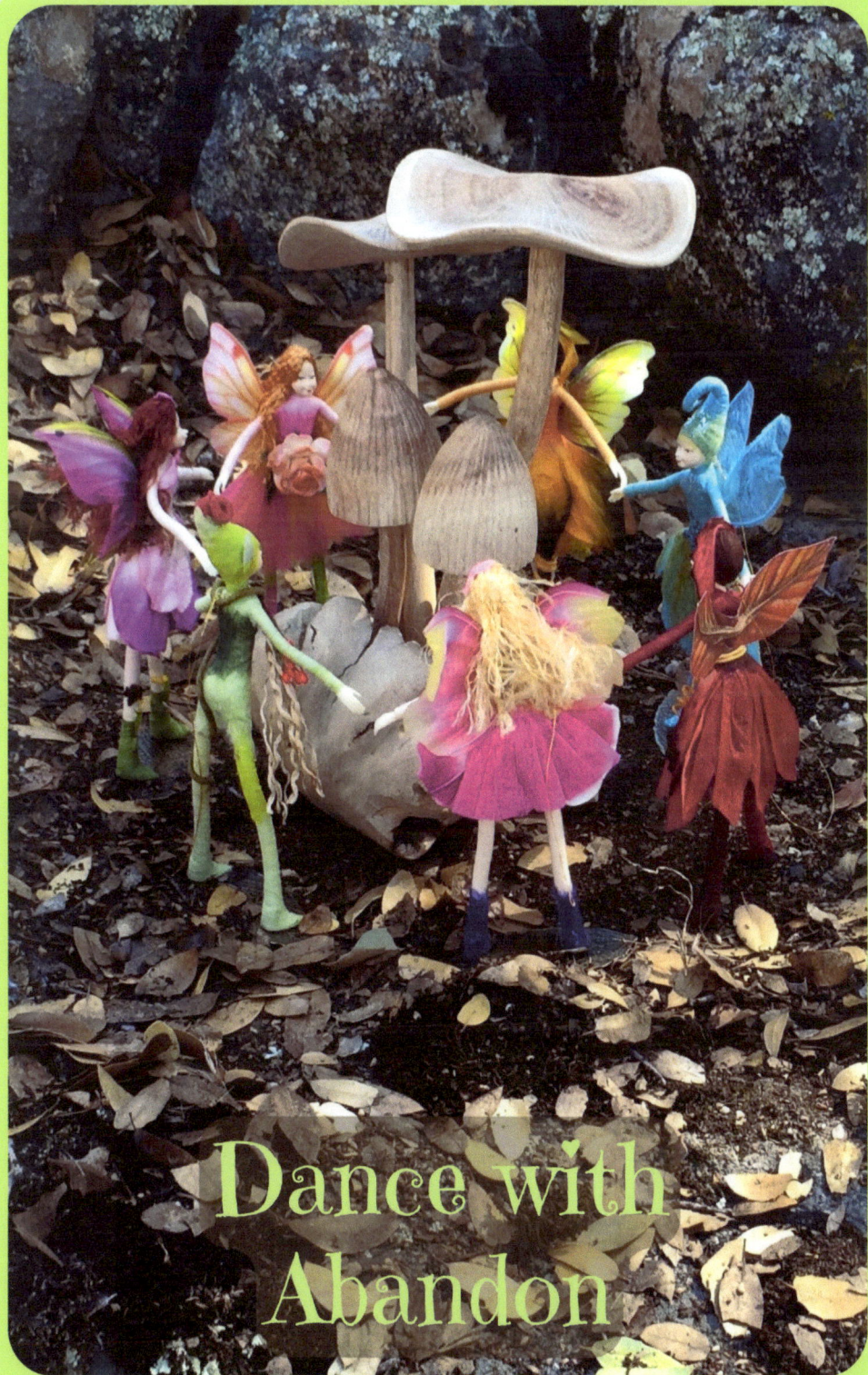

# Dance with Abandon

Don't be afraid to open new doors, even if others have yet to close. There is always something new – and generally unexpected - waiting for you on the other side. Fairies recognize the magic of doors and use them to move between realms.

# Open New Doors

Our planet and its abundant resources should never be taken for granted. Fairies have always followed the principles of Reduce, Reuse, and Recycle and always give back more than they take from the earth. Follow their lead.

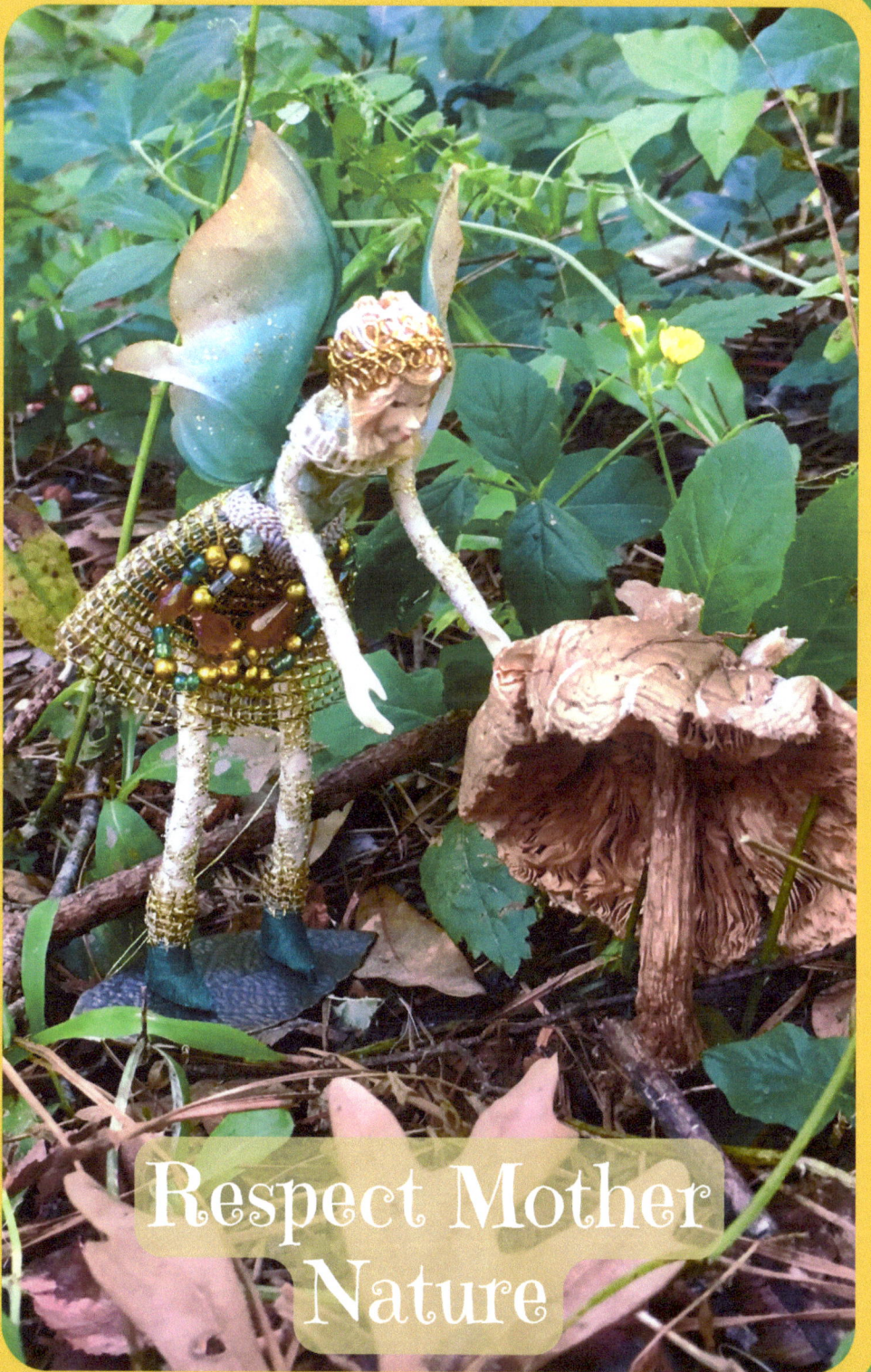

Respect Mother
Nature

Some people resist change, but it's a natural part of the life cycle. Each of the four season brings new experiences. Fairies love to assist with the seasonal transitions. Even if you live somewhere that only has one or two seasons, it's important to honor the passing of the year.

Welcome the Changes of the Seasons

Everyone has gifts, whether mental or physical or emotional. Some are obvious, some seem hidden. Work to uncover your talents. Sometimes what we perceive as our shortcomings are actually our greatest strengths. Embrace your individual gifts and those of your peers, just like the Fairies do.

# Honor Your Gifts

Fairies know that the world would be incredibly dull if everything and everyone were the same. We should all value, respect, and try to understand those different than us. Whether it's a human or another sentient being, we are all from this world.

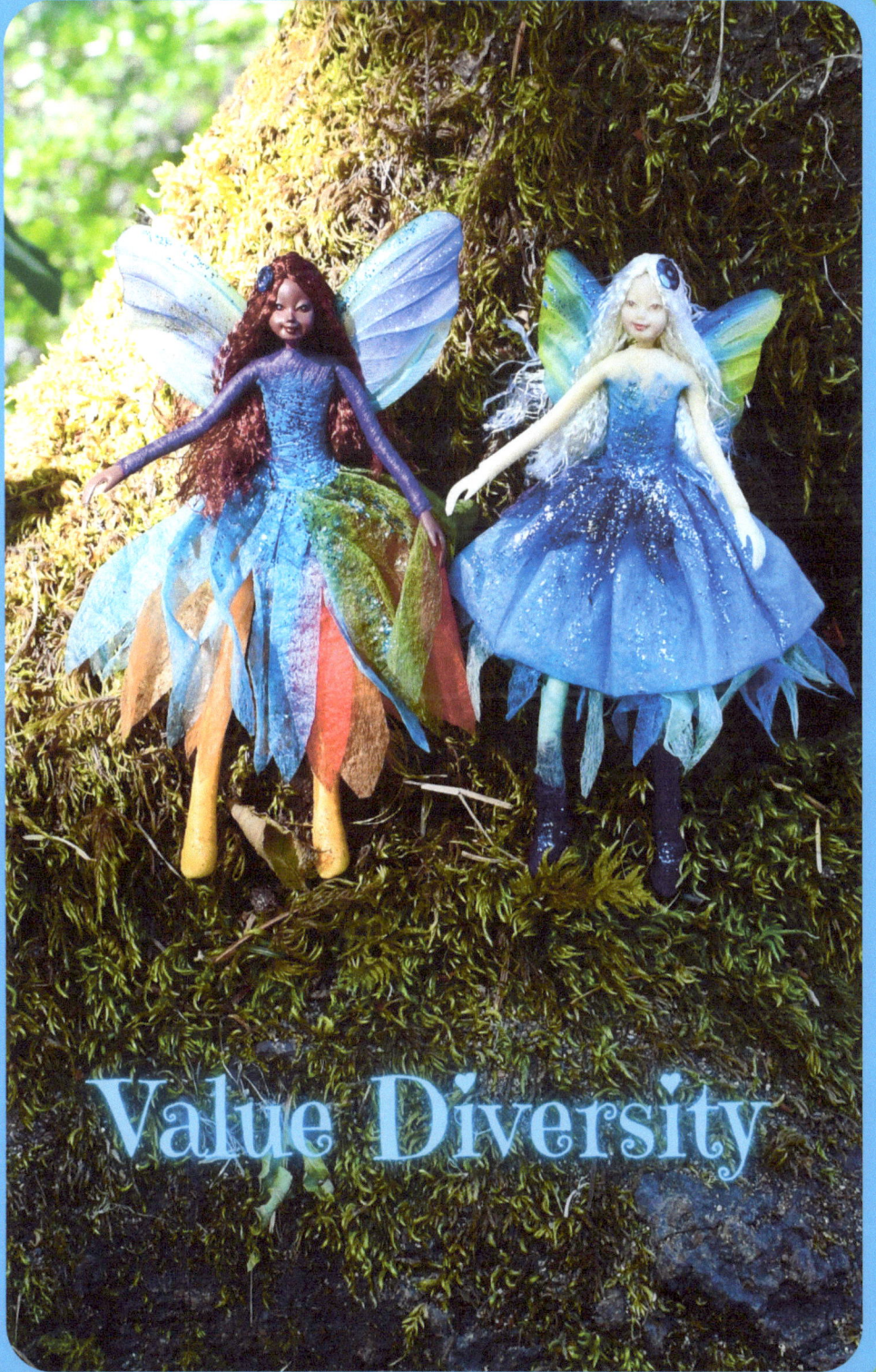

# Value Diversity

Since Beauty is the physical equivalent of Love, by noticing and appreciating the Beauty that exists all around you, you will be able to tap into the Love that surrounds you. To live like a Fairy is to perceive Love and Beauty in everything.

# Appreciate Beauty

This is so basic that the Fairies don't understand any other way. It distresses them greatly when they observe a human behaving less than kind to any other living being. A little kindness may go a long way, but big kindnesses have great Karmic rewards.

# Be Kind to Others

Fairies know that nature can be volatile, but even after a storm the sun will shine again. In difficult times remember that it is only temporary and try to find the lessons to be learned – or as the Fairies would say – always look for the rainbow.

# Weather the
# Storms

Adventure awaits those who are willing to break from the crowds and follow their own paths. Fairies embody this spirit of independence, always flying off in directions unknown, yet they always find their way home.

# Take the Roads Less Traveled

Fairies are masters of disguise and at blending in to go unnoticed. But they aren't afraid to reveal their true colors when they want. They encourage you to be bright.
Be beautiful.
Let your inner sparkle shine!

# Be Colorful

Never be afraid to ask for help when needed. It's impossible for one person to do everything alone. We all need to help each other. In the Fairy realm, asking for help is seen as a courageous act that boosts the strength of the Flutter.

# Ask for Help

Einstein said that there are two ways to live: to see nothing as a miracle, or everything as a miracle. Fairies see everything in nature as a miracle. The next time you watch a bee flying or a flower blooming, try to see the world through their eyes.

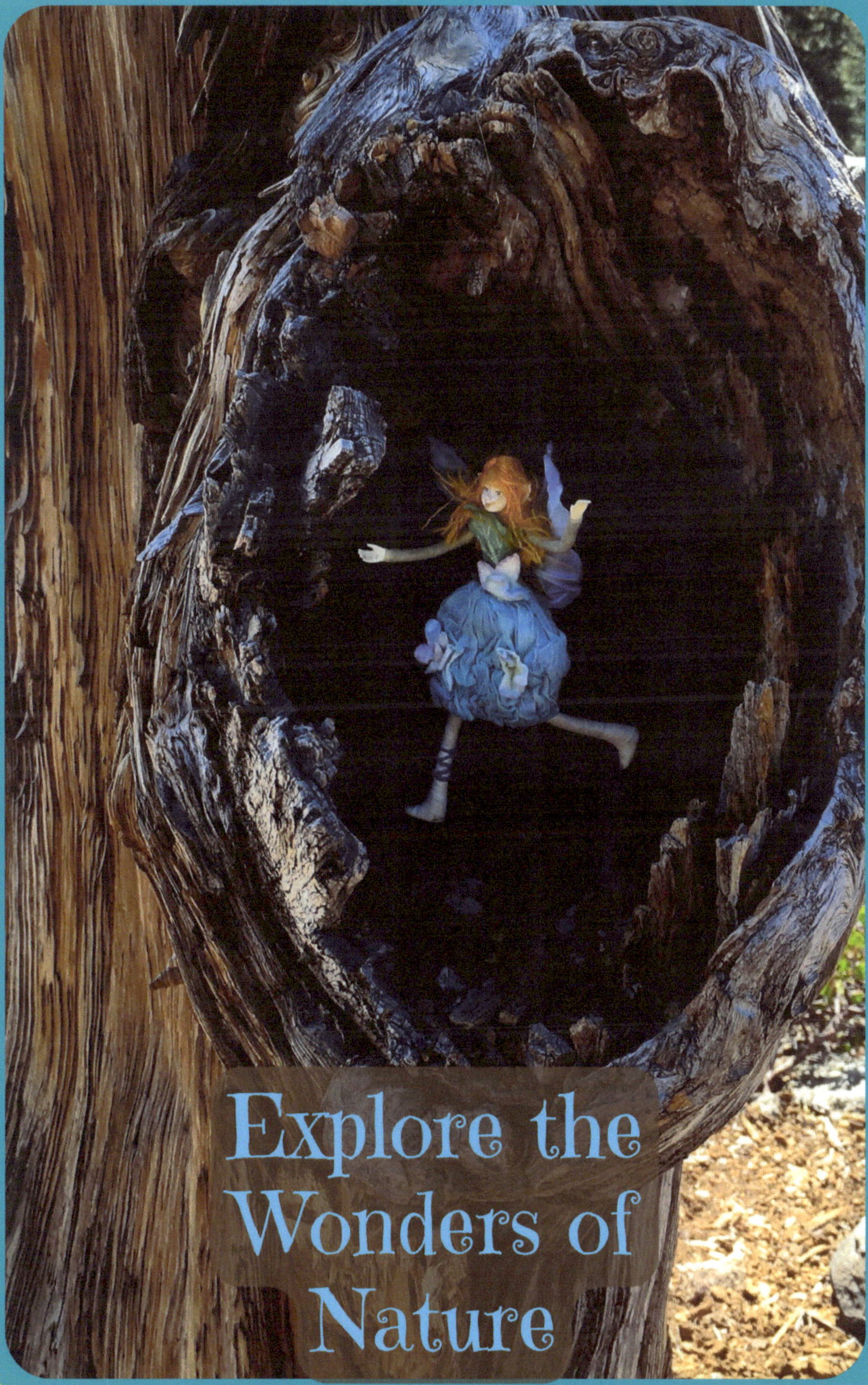

# Explore the Wonders of Nature

The Universe is constantly sending out signs, but we are usually too busy or too proud to notice. Some signs are in-your-face obvious, but most are more subtle and require our full attention. Fairies know that paying attention to signs will lead to living an easier life.

# Watch for Signs

Never hide your true
nature. No-one is the same,
so don't try to be like
every-one. Embrace your
differences even if they
seem like weaknesses.
Fairies love to stand tall –
even though they're small.

# Be Proud of
# What You Are

Nature offers surprises daily: Mushroom rings popping up overnight; Flowers blooming only in the sunshine. Fairies have a hand in all these changes, and love it when humans notice. Be aware of your surroundings and you might just spot something magical!

# Look Daily for Surprises

The Sun gives all of life its energy. We would not survive without it. Don't hide from the sun, but enjoy it. Fairies encourage you to watch the sun at sunrise or sunset. That is when they help paint the glorious colors in the sky.

# Get Plenty of Sunshine

Truth is of utmost importance –
but how do you discern what is
true when there are so many
conflicting opinions? By educating
yourself, and trusting yourself. The
Fairies encourage everyone to be
guided in their learning by listening
through their hearts.

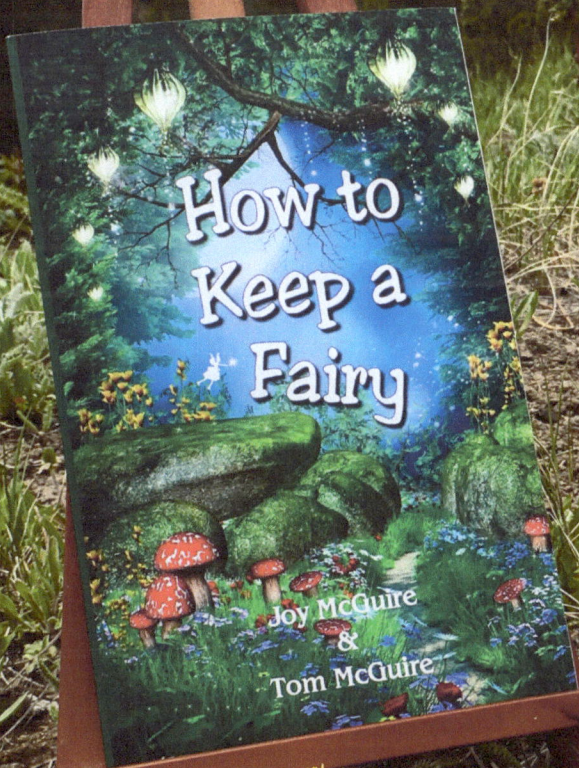

# Educate Yourself

How to
Keep a
Fairy

Joy McGuire
&
Tom McGuire

We can't all live in a treehouse in a forest. (Lucky are those who can!) But we can all spend as much time in nature as possible. The more time spent in nature, the wiser one becomes. Plus, your chances of glimpsing a fairy are increased.

# Immerse Yourself in Nature

Families give us strength and understanding. Whether your family is the one you were born into or one you have chosen, be thankful for their presence in your life. Fairy families are forever.

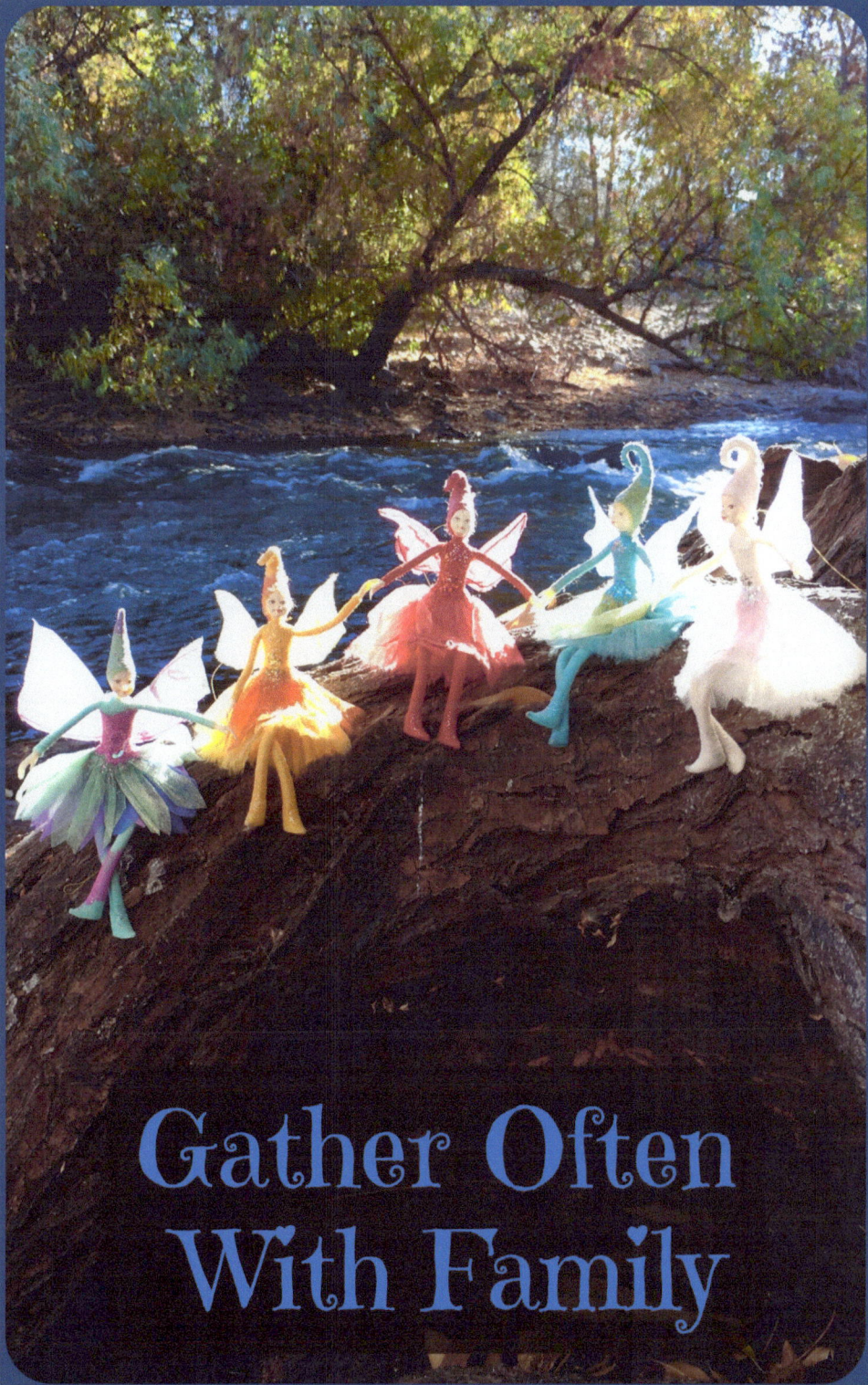

# Gather Often With Family

Beauty is the physical manifestation of Love. It exists all around us, from the tiniest of spaces to the plainest of places. All we need to do is look for it. Fairies understand this connection and that is why they are such loving beings.

# Search for Beauty

Would Fairies even exist if they didn't live in our imaginations? When we imagine, we live in creativity. When we live in creativity, we are able to create the world we desire.

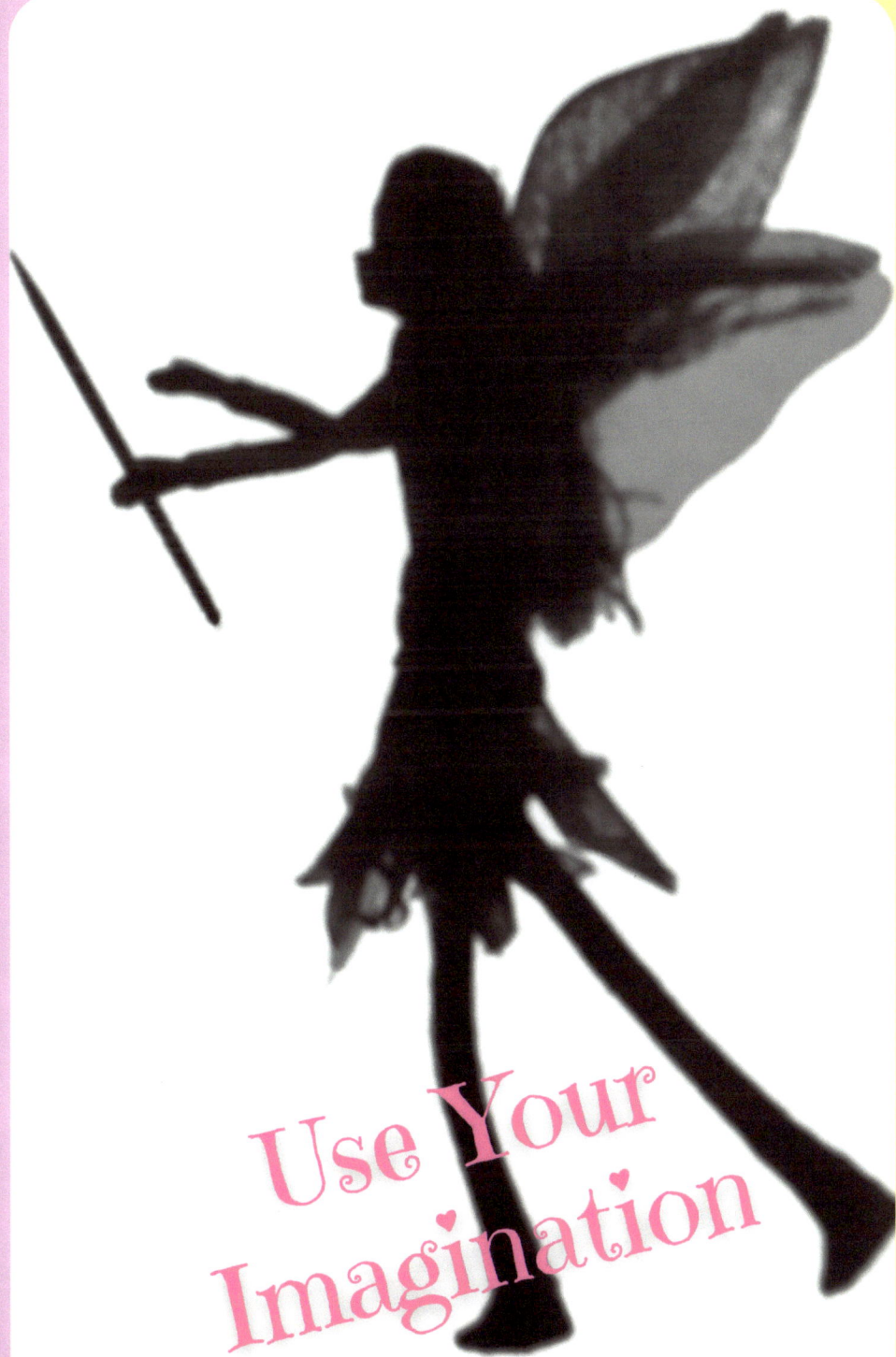

Use Your
Imagination

Fairies have a hard time with this one! They recognize the value of adding fun and games to our lives. However, there's a fine line between playful shenanigans and outright chaos. So for a better life, steer clear of trouble.

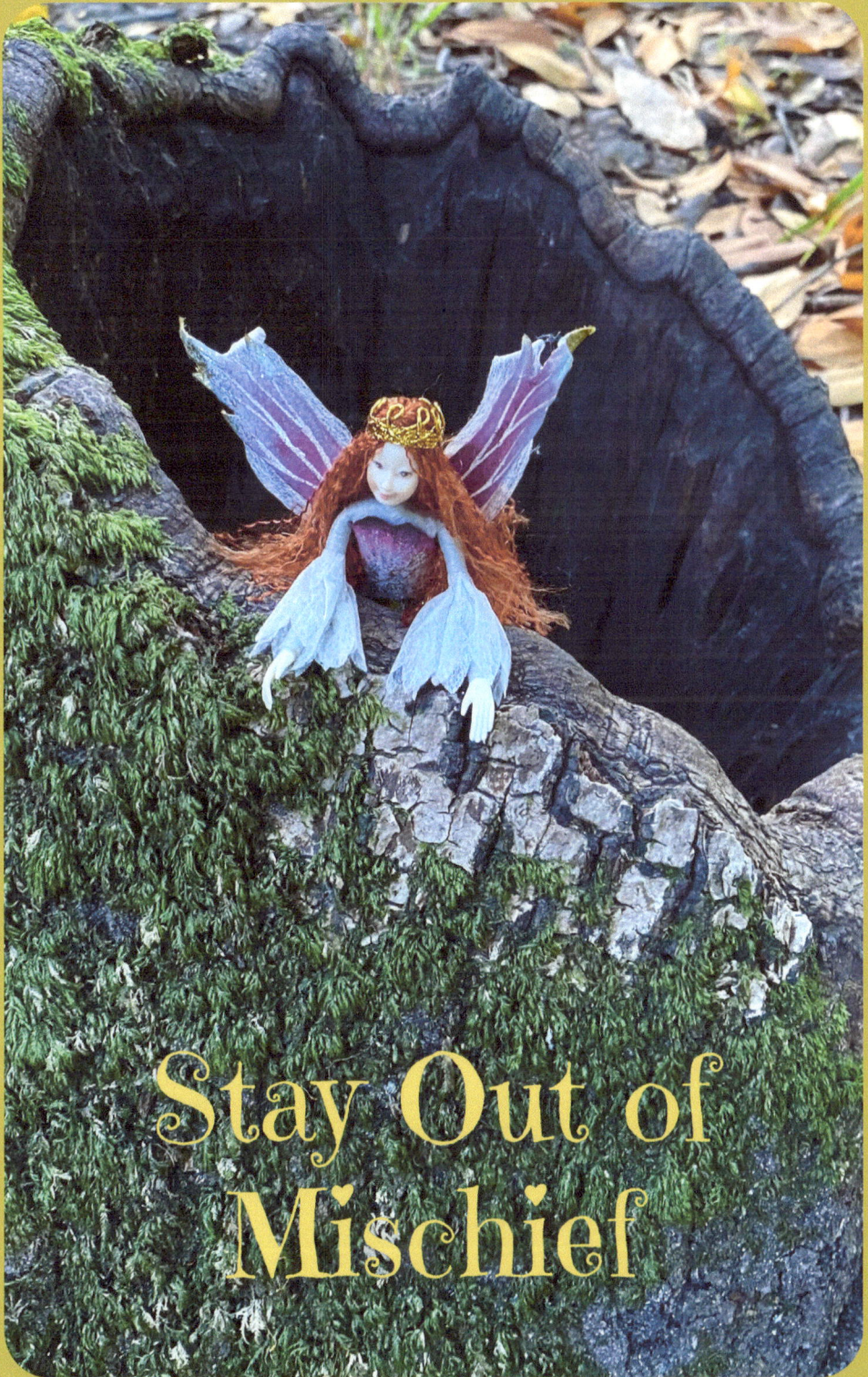

# Stay Out of Mischief

The primary purpose of Fairies is to take care of Nature, but they need our help. Humans can be very destructive. We all need to do what we can to ensure the beauty of our earth.

# Take Care of Nature

By now you know that Beauty and Nature exist everywhere – you just need to have eyes to see. Make a point of utilizing all of your senses to discover the beauty in everything.

# Find Beauty Everywhere

Believe in Magic! The Fairies are ever so grateful when you do. Open your heart and let down your guard and you will encounter the magic that exists – not just in the Fairy Realm but in the human world as well.

# Believe in Magic

# Dearest Reader,

*Thank you* so much for taking your time to look at this book. Whether you are young or young at heart, I appreciate your willingness to listen to the advice of the Fairies.

I hope you enjoyed the pictures and the lessons. Perhaps they gave you inspiration or food for thought. Are you ready to live like a Fairy now?

It would be ever so wonderful if you would leave an honest review of this book on Amazon.com.

Feel free to contact me at 559-972-7780 or at faefolkworld@gmail.com.

*Peace & Love, Joy*

# Positive Affirmation
## Page Number Index

# About the Author

Joy McGuire is a lifelong reader and award-winning writer.

After publishing two chick-lit novels, she turned her attention to lighter fare and began writing family-friendly, fairy-themed books.

She hopes to inspire imaginative thinking, appreciation of nature, hope, and of course, love – a theme present in all of her books. Her motto for life is "Love is the Answer".

This is her third book featuring photos of her Fae Folk® Fairies taken in nature settings across the country. The first was an 'instructional' book on taking care of fairies, and the second was a trilogy of tales from the fairies themselves.

She also has an online store where she sells these fairies at FaeFolkWorld.com.

**Also see them on:**

www.ingramcontent.com/pod-product-compliance
Lightning Source LLC
Chambersburg PA
CBHW041531090426
42738CB00036B/116